THIS BOOK BELONGS TO

[illegible]

[illegible]

Made in the USA
Monee, IL
04 March 2022

92263858R00070